W9-CEL-663

Kangaroo Island

A Story of an Australian Mallee Forest

The
Nature
Conservancy®

For Sasha, who explored Australia with me,
and for my parents, just because. — D.L.

For my son Isaac,
who wants to draw kangaroos. — F.O.

Book copyright © 1998 Trudy Corporation, 353 Main Avenue, Norwalk, CT 06851.

Soundprints is a division of Trudy Corporation, Norwalk, Connecticut.

Book Design: Diane Hinze Kanzler

First Edition 1998
10 9 8 7 6 5 4 3 2 1
Printed in Hong Kong

Acknowledgements:
   Our very special thanks to Peggy and Mike McKelvey of the Pelican Lagoon Research and Wildlife Centre on Kangaroo Island for their review and guidance. Thanks also to Rooby and Jumper, the Centre's resident 'roos, for being such good models!

Library of Congress Cataloging-in-Publication Data

Langeland, Deidre, 1973–

   Kangaroo Island: story of an Australian mallee forest / by Deidre Langeland ; illustrated by Frank Ordaz.
         p.   cm.
   Summary: As morning comes to Kangaroo Island following a thunderstorm, a mother kangaroo finds her lost baby and a burned eucalyptus tree sprouts buds and becomes a new home for animals.
      ISBN 1-56899-543-1 (hardcover)   ISBN 1-56899-544-X (pbk.)
   1. Western grey kangaroo — Juvenile fiction.   2. Kangaroo Island (S. Aust.) — Juvenile fiction. [1. Western grey kangaroo — Fiction.   2. Kangaroos — Fiction. 3. Kangaroo Island (S. Aust.) — Fiction.   4. Australia — Fiction.   5. Zoology — Australia — Fiction.   6. Forest ecology — Fiction.   7. Ecology — Fiction]   I. Ordaz, Frank, 1956– ill.   II. Title.
         PZ10.3.L345Kan 1998   97-47612
         [Fic] — dc21   CIP
                                                                                   AC

Kangaroo Island

A Story of an Australian Mallee Forest

by Deidre Langeland
Illustrated by Frank Ordaz

Soundprints
Where Children Discover...

It is summer, and December sun bathes Kangaroo Island, off the coast of Adelaide, South Australia. All winter long, cold Antarctic winds and waters crashed against the island's rugged cliffs. Now, Australian sea lions bask on the shores of Seal Bay, barking to each other. Fairy penguins glide beneath the waves, hunting for fish.

From far out at sea, a white-breasted sea-eagle flies home on six-foot wings. It sails to its nest on the rocky cliffs that are dotted with a low eucalyptus shrub called mallee.

In the mallee scrub, different sounds fill the air. Crickets hum and a rainbow lorikeet flutters from one mallee blossom to another.

Beneath a twenty-foot scribbly gum tree, a mob of kangaroos waits silently in the shade. When the sun sets, the mob will venture out of the forest in search of grass to eat. But now it is too hot. The male kangaroo licks his forelegs to cool off.

Beside him, five does lie beneath the mallee. Three of them have babies, called joeys. Sometimes they drowse in the afternoon heat. Most of the time they listen. Their long ears flick forward and back as an echidna tears at a rotted log in a search for termites.

Low thunder rumbles across the island. The kangaroos' ears prick to alert. A storm is coming.

Soon, dusk settles. Glossy-black cockatoos ride the salty evening wind on their way to a sugar gum tree to settle down for the night. Their noisy passage wakes some of the bush dwellers that have been sleeping. A bright-eyed pygmy possum is the first to appear, reaching for a banksia flower to start his evening meal.

Throughout the forest, nighttime animals begin to stir. A brushtail possum pokes her soft pink nose into the night air and sniffs the dampness of the storm. Flashes of lightning show the silhouettes of long-eared bats as they head out from the trees.

With the darkness, the kangaroos leave
the forest for the fields of the nearby farmland.
They make their way slowly. Balancing on their
small forelegs and tails, they swing their long
back legs forward and take a big step, rocking
back like a see-saw. Then they lean forward
to begin another step. Gusts of wind ruffle their
woolly brown fur. The grass is dry and brittle.
It has been a long time since the last rain.

The kangaroos move to a billabong —
the grass is tastier near the tiny waterhole.
As the does nibble on tender shoots, their joeys
stretch to try the strange food. Through the
spring they have nursed in their mothers'
pouches. Only recently have they started to eat
grass and leaves.

One nine-month-old joey is large enough to graze on his own. He moves away from the mob toward the water's edge.

He surprises a platypus, who slips from the muddy bank to glide below the water. The platypus's broad bill moves back and forth across the bottom. It scoops up worms, insects, and shellfish, along with pebbles and mud. When its cheek-pouches are full, the platypus swims to the far shore to enjoy its dinner.

Then, with a loud crack, lightning strikes a tall gum tree. The mob of kangaroos is off, bounding across the grassland with long, panicked leaps. The mothers are slowed down, keeping pace with their young, but still they cover ten feet in a bound. The male kangaroo stamps his foot to warn the adventurous joey. The joey dashes after them, but he cannot keep up.

The gum tree catches fire quickly. A burning branch drops to the forest floor, spreading flames through the dry leaves. The fire burns hot and fast, feeding on the fragrant oil of stringybark.

The smaller branches and leaves of the trees are quickly eaten up by the fire, but the tough bark of their trunks resists. The heart of the tree is safe. Hot air rises from the flames, carrying sparks, ashes, and seeds with it. On the forest floor, the tough seed cases of many of the trees split open with the heat.

Thick smoke drifts from the trees toward the grass. The joey leaps away from the danger of the fire, springing through the grass. A tammar wallaby almost runs into him as it bolts from the shelter of the scrub. Confused, the young kangaroo stops. He scans the night for his mob, but sees nothing. Smoky wind stings his eyes.

Soon the rain comes. First a few drops, then more and more until the frightened joey is drenched in cold water. He huddles beneath yacca fronds, tired and trembling with cold and fear. The fire has quickly burned up the eucalyptus leaves and does not have fuel to last through the downpour. It begins to sputter and die.

With the first gray light of dawn, a calm settles over the mallee. Possums and birds begin to search for new homes. The wallaby creeps back to the scrub to rest.

A soft muzzle reaches into the yacca fronds and stretches to touch the joey. His mother has found him! The kangaroos, fur matted and heavy with rain, slip into the shelter of a stand of trees that was not touched by the fire.

The burned section of forest stands bare. The fire has left sooty scars on the trunks of trees, and many have dropped branches in the heat and wind. Ash and seeds are scattered everywhere. Everything is black — the tree trunks, the branches, the forest floor. But, beneath the charred bark of the trees, new buds are already waiting. The forest will survive.

Within weeks, the buds grow into delicate red and green shoots. Possums rebuild their nests, and birds move into hollows made by fallen branches. Even termites find new homes. The scarred, black bark on the trees is now easy to break through—before the fire, it would have been too hard. Whole termite colonies begin to move into the trees, where they soon make hollows big enough for larger animals of the forest to make a home.

In the rich ash that coats the forest floor, seeds cracked by the heat begin to sprout. Tiny plants that will one day be proud gum and slow-growing yacca trees peek from beneath the soot.

Fire is a rare visitor to Kangaroo Island, but without fire's help, the mallee could not thrive.

Deep reds and purples stretch across the sky and the cockatoos chatter on their way home. Bright-eyed possums and bandicoots rustle through the forest. The wind tosses dangling leaves. The Australian night settles in, clear and cool.

In the darkness of the grassland, an inky sky is thick with stars. As the Southern Cross creeps over the horizon, the kangaroos make their slow, see-sawing way through the grass, nibbling on the tender shoots that have sprung up. By now, all the joeys wander on their own, but not too far from their mothers—just in case!

Kangaroo Island, South Australia

Kangaroo Island is located southwest of Adelaide, off the coast of
South Australia. The island is home to a number of national parks that
protect many endangered species.

About Kangaroo Island

In 1802, a British explorer named Matthew Flinders discovered a large island—90 miles long and 32 miles wide—southwest of what is now Adelaide, off the coast of South Australia. He saw so many kangaroos there that he called it Kangaroo Island. The kangaroo from which the island got its name is the western gray kangaroo. At its full height, a western gray kangaroo can be between five and six feet tall.

Kangaroo Island is home to a number of national parks that protect many endangered species. Ten percent of the Australian sea lions left in the world are sheltered there, as well as rare, glossy-black cockatoos.

Most of the mammals that live on Kangaroo Island are marsupials. These animals give birth to tiny, hairless babies that live and nurse inside pouches on their mothers' stomachs until they grow fur and are big enough to start living outside the pouch. Kangaroos, wallabies and possums are marsupials native to Kangaroo Island. Two marsupials not native to the island, koalas and wombats, were introduced in the 1920s. The wombats did not survive in the new habitat, but there are now so many koalas that they are upsetting the ecological balance.

The trees found on Kangaroo Island are mostly eucalypts. Their thick bark and waxy leaves help the trees hold in moisture during the hot Australian summer (December through February). In a fire, the leaves of the tree burn quickly, but the tough bark protects the trunk, where special buds wait. After the fire, these buds poke through the damaged bark and within days the tree is growing again. Some eucalypts even depend on fire to help them reproduce. Their seeds have such thick coats, they need the heat and the smoke gasses of a fire to crack them open so they can sprout.

While forest fires are frightening for animals and people, they are also a valuable part of forest ecology. Fires clear away dead plants and undergrowth, burst open seed cases, leave ash that fertilizes the soil, and make hollows in which birds and small animals can live.

Glossary

▲ *Australian sea lions*

▲ *Correa bush*

▲ *Glossy-black cockatoo*

▲ *Bush-tail possum*

▲ *Fairy penguin*

▲ *Mallee eucalyptus*

▲ *Burr daisy*

▲ *Rainbow lorikeet*

▲ *Billibong*

▲ *Joey*

▲ *Western gray kangaroo*

▲ *Duck-billed platypus*

▲ *Lesser long-eared bat*

▲ *Western pygmy possum*

▲ *Echidna*

▲ *Tammar wallaby*

▲ *Yacca grass tree*